PONDICHERRY
UNVEILED

(A 2024 PONDICHERRY TRAVEL GUIDE)

A Tapestry of History, Spirituality, and Coastal Charm

TOM ALBERT

No part of this book may be copied or
transmitted in any way, whether
electronically or mechanically, including
by photocopying, recording, or using
any information storage and retrieval
system, without the express consent
of the publisher.

TABLE OF CONTENTS

INTRODUCTION

Welcome to the charming town of Pondicherry, a seaside retreat that skillfully combines a strong French influence with the intricate fabric of Indian heritage. When you set out on your adventure through the Pondicherry Travel Guide 2024, be ready to be enthralled by a place that exists outside of time and presents a unique blend of spirituality, history, and contemporary charm.

The Bay of Bengal borders Pondicherry, commonly referred to as Puducherry, a Union Territory on India's southeast coast. Entering this charming town seems like stepping through a gateway where the dynamic energy of the present blends with the echoes of the past. With the help of our guide, discover Pondicherry's many layers, intriguing stories, and undiscovered jewels.

Pondicherry's history is a fascinating tale that emerges from its colonial past. The town's architecture, food, and manner of life were all profoundly influenced by its history as the capital of French India in the 18th century, when it was still a French trade station. When you stroll along the enchanting streets, you'll notice a smooth fusion of French and Tamil influences, which are evident in the colonial-era buildings, the alleyways lined with bougainvillea, and the modest cafés that have a certain European elegance.

Cultural enthusiasts will be able to immerse themselves in a wealth of spiritual and creative experiences. The well-known Auroville, an experimental community devoted to spiritual advancement and human harmony, is located in Pondicherry. Founded by Sri Aurobindo and The Mother, the Aurobindo Ashram welcomes travelers from all over the globe, providing a peaceful environment for reflection and meditation. Temples, churches, and mosques are interwoven throughout the town's varied fabric, symbolizing the peaceful coexistence of many religious groups.

Pondicherry has immaculate beaches that are conducive to relaxation and reflection for anyone seeking comfort by the sea. The famous Promenade Beach is a popular location for leisurely strolls as the sun sets over the Bay of Bengal because of its colorful shoreline and colonial monuments. Go a bit further and you'll find the remote Paradise Beach, which is only reachable by boat and is surrounded by peaceful, unspoiled beauty.

Enjoying the regional cuisine is an essential part of every trip, and Pondicherry offers delicious local cuisine. Savor French and South Indian food combined in a way that showcases the town's many influences. From lively street food booths to upscale restaurants offering exquisite seafood and French pastries, this tour will show you the hidden culinary jewels.

Pondicherry extends a warm greeting to all travelers, whether they are history buffs, adventure seekers, or peace-seekers. This book will be your traveling companion, offering advice, suggestions, and insider knowledge to make sure your trip around Pondicherry is nothing short of spectacular. So grab a seat, and get ready to be engrossed in Pondicherry's charm, where every street has a tale to tell and every corner begs you to make up your own.

DISCOVERING PONDICHERRY

An Exploration of Culture and Time

You are about to embark on an experience through time and culture that goes beyond simple travel as you enter the heart of Pondicherry. The town of Pondicherry is revealed via the pages of the Pondicherry Travel Guide 2024, where ethnic variety is intertwined into everyday life and history is spoken through cobblestone streets.

The Past and Traditions

The tale of Pondicherry's past is revealed as it turns like the pages of an old book. The town's history dates back to the Pallava Kingdom in the second century. But the French East India Company's establishment of a trade presence here in the 17th century marked a turning point. Over the next few years, Pondicherry developed into a colonial gem, with a noticeable French influence.

You'll find a visual feast of colonial-era buildings while strolling around White Town. The Tamil Quarter's vivid colors contrast with the charming mustard-yellow houses with balconies wrapped in bougainvillea. The French Quarter transports you to a bygone age when Pondicherry was the capital of French India with its quaint residences and well maintained buildings.

Cultural Highlights

Pondicherry is a painting created with a variety of ethnic brushstrokes. The town's cultural attractions, each telling a unique tale, are the heartbeat of the community. The spiritual center is the Aurobindo Ashram, which was established by Sri Aurobindo and The Mother. Its calm atmosphere provides comfort to visitors, who meditate and reflect there.

The progressive ethos of the area is exemplified by Auroville, an experimental community devoted to human harmony. Transcendence is exuded by the Matrimandir, the famous golden sphere in the center of Auroville. It's a location where individuals from all over the world converge to pursue a peaceful life.

Architecture and Landmarks

The architecture of Pondicherry is an intriguing fusion of West and East. With its imposing neo-Gothic style, the Basilica of the Sacred Heart of Jesus commands attention. The Raj Niwas, on the other hand, emanates colonial grandeur and was once the house of the French Governors. Offering sweeping views of the Bay of Bengal, the town's lighthouse serves as both a working beacon and a reminder of Pondicherry's nautical past.

Past these attractions, the town's streets are dotted with bustling marketplaces, churches from the colonial period, and historically significant structures that beg to be explored. Every edifice beckons you to enter a bygone period, and every nook tells a tale.

A Visit to the Beaches

The shoreline of Pondicherry is a painting that nature has painted with shades of adventure and peace. Popular with both inhabitants and visitors is Promenade Beach, a busy stretch along the town. The music for leisurely walks is the rhythmic crash of waves on the coast. When dusk falls, the beach becomes a bustling community hub where residents participate in a variety of activities.

A contrast is provided by Paradise Beach, which is reachable by boat. Here, you may find a quiet sanctuary where the only noises are the wind and the waves. Another hidden treasure waiting to be discovered is Auroville Beach, which has golden beaches and a tranquil ambiance. Pondicherry's beaches are suitable for all types of people, whether you choose to be alone or with others.

With its distinct fusion of culture, history, and scenic beauty, Pondicherry beckons you to explore its many facets and take in an extraordinary experience. As your compass, the Pondicherry Travel Guide 2024 leads you through the many attractions this seaside resort has to offer. Put on your walking shoes, let the scents and hues of the streets fill your senses, and allow Pondicherry to reveal itself to you. This place is where exploration becomes more than simply a trip; it's a celebration of the classic and the modern, intertwined in a way that only a local could.

PONDICHERRY'S DIVERSE BEACHES

A Look Inside Their Coastal Charms

Travelers are enticed to explore the coastal beauty that adorns Pondicherry's coasts by the city's attraction, which reaches far beyond its ancient streets and cultural sites. The sun-kissed stretches are covered in detail in a chapter of The Pondicherry Travel Guide 2024, which invites you to see the many beaches that are evidence of the town's coastline splendor.

The Promenade Beach

Promenade Beach is without a doubt the center of Pondicherry's coastal appeal. Encircling the town's eastern boundary, this vibrant beachfront offers a unique fusion of local culture, leisure, and history. People go to the Promenade for energizing walks and jogs as the early light creates a pleasant glow on the beaches.

Promenade Beach is distinguished by its distinct promenade, which is a sidewalk with pavement running along to the beach. You'll come across monuments honoring historical personalities and significant occasions as you go along. Two quiet witnesses to the town's growth are the renowned Mahatma Gandhi monument and the historic lighthouse.

The atmosphere changes when day gives way to darkness. The smell of salt fills the sea wind as street sellers open up business, selling a wide range of food and souvenirs. The promenade turns into a bustling stage for cultural events as locals get together for evening talks. More than simply a location, Promenade Beach is a dynamic painting that captures Pondicherry's spirit.

The Paradise Beach

A quick boat trip from Chunnambar Boat House brings visitors to the immaculate sands of Paradise Beach, ideal for those seeking a more sedate seaside experience. A sense of suspense grows as the boat slips through the backwaters, surrounded by verdant mangroves. An isolated paradise of golden beaches gently hugged by the Bay of Bengal, Paradise Beach is nothing short of beautiful from the first look.

Seeking solitude? Paradise Beach is a haven unspoiled by commercialization. The sounds of the rustling palm leaves and the waves are all that are audible. It's a spot to relax, read a book under a coconut tree, or just take in the view of the horizon as your feet are massaged by the smooth sand. The calm atmosphere of the beach provides a well-rounded coastal experience within the boundaries of Pondicherry, in sharp contrast to the lively activity of Promenade Beach.

Auroville Beach

Another hidden treasure that's worth exploring is Auroville Beach, which is tucked away between the settlement of Auroville and the Bay of Bengal. This beach, which is accessible by short car or bicycle ride, provides a special fusion of spiritual emotions and natural beauty. The beach's atmosphere is enhanced as you get closer by the architectural wonder of Auroville Matrimandir, which sits in the background like a quiet protector.

Both residents and tourists use Auroville Beach as a canvas on which to paint their tales. The calming music produced by the repetitive waves encourages reflection and relaxation. Yoga devotees frequent the beach, drawn by the peace and quiet that permeates the region. For those looking for a comprehensive beach experience, it's a must-visit location as it offers a space for self-connection with nature.

There is a certain allure to every beach in Pondicherry, one that suits every mood and taste. Pondicherry's coastline is varied and welcoming, offering something for everyone to enjoy, whether they are attracted to the lively energy of Promenade Beach, the peaceful isolation of Paradise Beach, or the spiritual ambience of Auroville Beach.

Useful Advice for Beach Exploration

A few useful pointers should be kept in mind while you take in Pondicherry's coastline wonders:

1. Sun Protection: The sun around the shore may be strong, so remember to protect yourself with sunscreen, a hat, and sunglasses.

2. Hydration: Drink plenty of water, particularly if you'll be at the beach for a long time. Reduce your influence on the environment by carrying a reusable water bottle.

3. Footwear: Having comfortable shoes is essential, particularly if you want to visit many beaches. Sand beaches are the perfect place for flip-flops.

4. Respect Local Norms: Recognize and adhere to local laws and traditions. Certain beaches could have particular rules for things like swimming and photography.

5. Waste Management: Make responsible waste disposal choices to maintain the cleanliness of the beaches. If you happen to produce any trash, think about bringing a little bag to collect it.

You are immersing yourself in a timeless story where the sea, sand, and sun come together to produce once-in-a-lifetime experiences as you explore Pondicherry's beaches. As you explore these coastal treasures, each providing a distinct chapter in the history of this enthralling town, let the Pondicherry Travel Guide 2024 be your guide.

A CULINARY ODYSSEY

Pondicherry's Diverse Cuisine

Take a gastronomic tour across Pondicherry's bustling streets, where each dish has a backstory and each taste is a harmonious blend of many cultural influences. A chapter on the town's culinary offerings appears in The Pondicherry Travel Guide 2024, beckoning you to indulge in the blend of French and South Indian cuisines that characterize the town's culinary scene.

Regional Cuisine

The distinctive fusion of tastes that resulted from the blending of French and Tamil culinary traditions is the essence of Pondicherry's culinary tapestry. This harmonic blend is evident in the town's unique cuisine, which offers a wide variety of delicacies that entice the palate.

With a steamy cup of sambar, a South Indian lentil soup flavored with fragrant spices, begin your culinary journey. Enjoy it with fluffy idli or crunchy dosa for a classic Tamil breakfast. The neighborhood booths and little restaurants that line the streets sell these genuine South Indian specialties are well-known to the residents.

If you go further into the winding lanes, you'll come across bakeries and cafés with a French influence. Savor a leisurely breakfast here, complete with buttery croissants, pain au chocolat, and robust, fragrant coffee. The contrast between French pastries and street cuisine from South India perfectly captures the exquisite gastronomic variety that is Pondicherry.

Well-known eateries

There are plenty of eateries in Pondicherry that provide a well selected eating experience for those with different tastes. Wandering around the French Quarter will reveal you quaint bistros and upscale restaurants where chefs create gastronomic works of art that highlight the town's distinct fusion of influences.

Situated in a mansion from the colonial period, Le Dupleix provides a sophisticated dining experience with a cuisine that skillfully combines French methods with regional products. Popular with residents and visitors alike, the seafront Le Café on the Promenade is known for its laid-back vibe and wide selection of seafood dishes.

An outstanding meal influenced by traditional Chettinad cuisine is served at Maison Perumal, offering a contemporary take on Pondicherry's distinct tastes. The delicacies prepared by the chefs here are a celebration of Pondicherry's cultural richness, created with a deft fusion of French culinary refinement and regional flavors.

Delights of Street Food

A trip to Pondicherry would not be complete without sampling the thriving street food scene that lines the city's main thoroughfares and marketplaces. Head to Goubert Market, where street sellers tempt you with a mouthwatering selection of regional food.

Taste the zesty and piquant tastes of Pani Puri, a well-liked street snack made of crispy, hollow puris packed with a blend of potatoes, chickpeas, tamarind chutney, and flavored water. The perfume of freshly baked Bajjis, a savory fritter often prepared with onions or green chilies, fills the air, luring passerby to partake in this mouthwatering delight.

The streets of Pondicherry provide a lovely selection of delicacies for those who have a sweet appetite. Enjoy the melt-in-your-mouth flavor A classic South Indian dessert composed with gram flour, sugar, and ghee is called Mysore Pak. The town's bakeries showcase its French heritage, offering mouth watering pastries, macarons, and éclairs that are on par with those you may find on the streets of Paris.

Creating Memories Through Food

The goal of Pondicherry's culinary scene is to create experiences that create lasting taste memories, not only to satisfy hunger. Not only are you savoring the tastes as you relish each meal, but you're also losing yourself in the town's rich cultural story.

A trip through Pondicherry's food is an investigation of harmonies and contrasts, where the delicate refinement of French cuisine blends with the scorching spices of South India. It is an international symphony of tastes that invites you to savor a special combination that is distinctly Pondicherrian.

Utilitarian Advice for Culinary Adventures

1. Local Markets: For a real taste of street cuisine, visit nearby markets like Goubert Market.

2. Cafés and Bakeries: For a flavor of Pondicherry's French influence, don't miss the quaint cafés and bakeries in the French Quarter.

3. Seafood Exploration: Pondicherry is a coastline town, so take advantage of the variety of seafood selections served at different eateries.

4. Spice Appreciation: Savor the robust tastes of South Indian spices that are used in regional cuisine, and don't be afraid to ask for suggestions if you're not familiar with them.

5. Culinary Workshops: A few places provide culinary classes where you may learn how to make the special cuisine of Pondicherry. Inquire about availability and book ahead of time.

Let the Pondicherry Travel Guide 2024 be your guide as you explore the area's many gastronomic offerings; it will lead you through the maze-like maze of tastes that makes this seaside town a food lover's paradise. The gastronomic experiences offered by Pondicherry, which range from French-inspired treats to traditional South Indian cuisine, promise a culinary adventure as varied and rich as the town itself.

SPIRITUAL RETREATS IN PONDICHERRY

The town of Pondicherry, which is hugged by the Bay of Bengal, entices the traveler seeking a deep spiritual experience in addition to captivating with its stunning coastline. The Pondicherry Travel Guide 2024 opens with a chapter on the town's spiritual retreats, which provide comfort, reflection, and a feeling of transcendence to travelers from all over the globe.

Auroville

At the core of Pondicherry's spiritual appeal is Auroville, a cutting-edge city that goes beyond traditional ideas of spirituality and community. Auroville, which was created by architect Roger Anger and founded in 1968 by Mirra Alfassa, sometimes referred to as "The Mother," is a monument to the idea of human progress and oneness.

Not only is the Matrimandir, a circular golden structure in the center of Auroville, a wonder of architecture, but it also represents the town's spiritual center. The Matrimandir, which is surrounded by peaceful gardens, welcomes guests to enter its inner chamber, a calm area known as the Inner Chamber, for reflection and meditation. Its peaceful setting encourages a close relationship with one's inner self.

More than simply a location, Auroville is a living experiment where individuals from all walks of life come together to investigate sustainable development, alternative lifestyles, and spiritual development. The town's array of offerings, including meditation and yoga classes as well as cultural events, provide guests the opportunity to fully engage in an experience that goes beyond the norm.

Aurobindo Ashram

The Aurobindo Ashram, established in 1926 by the philosopher, poet, and yogi Sri Aurobindo, is a testament to Pondicherry's spiritual heritage. Situated in the center of the town, the ashram serves as a haven for those who are attracted to Sri Aurobindo and The Mother's teachings.

The actual remains of Sri Aurobindo and The Mother are housed in the Samadhi, a memorial shrine inside the ashram that is open to devotees and guests to pay their respects. The ashram's calm atmosphere, which includes meditation areas and shaded courtyards, fosters reflection and spiritual contemplation.

Collective meditation sessions, where individuals gather to participate in a quiet communion with the divine, are a daily activity at the Aurobindo Ashram. With its extensive selection of spiritual books, the ashram library is a valuable resource for anybody looking for a deep understanding of Sri Aurobindo's teachings.

Churches and Temples

Pondicherry's spiritual fabric is weaved not just by its historic churches and temples but also by its contemporary spiritual hubs. Lord Ganesha's temple, the

Arulmigu Manakula Vinayagar Temple, is a hallowed site of devotion where followers come to get blessings and comfort. The town's spiritual atmosphere is enhanced by the temple's vivid rituals and beautiful architecture.

The Basilica of the Sacred Heart of Jesus, a well-known church in Pondicherry's French Quarter, is another example of the city's rich spiritual variety and colonial past. The church's soaring spires and calm interiors beckon people to pause, think, and find some tranquility.

Utilitarian Guidance for Spiritual Discovery

1. Respectful Attire: Because spiritual locations are holy, it is best to dress modestly while visiting them.

2. Silence and Meditation: Savor the quiet of introspective periods. Many settings promote quiet contemplation, one of which is the Matrimandir in Auroville.

3. Participation in Activities: For a more immersive experience, think about taking advantage of the yoga or meditation classes that these spiritual retreats provide.

4. Cultural Sensitivity: Pay attention to the spiritual and cultural customs of the locations you visit. Learn about the traditions of the area to guarantee a civil and enlightening encounter.

Discovering Pondicherry's spiritual retreats reveals not only actual locations but also an intense feeling of unity - a unity with the cosmos, oneself, and the community spirit that pervades the town's spiritual environment. Let the Pondicherry go Guide 2024 be your guide as you go through the tranquil areas of Auroville, meditate silently at the Aurobindo Ashram, or find comfort in the historic churches and temples. It will lead you on a spiritual trip that goes beyond time and space.

PONDICHERRY'S OUTDOOR ADVENTURES

Setting Out on Pondicherry's Outdoor Playground

Adventure seekers are drawn to Pondicherry by its beautiful terrain and charming beachfront location. A chapter on outdoor activities appears in The Pondicherry Travel Guide 2024, beckoning you to experience the exhilaration of boat cruises, bike trips, and nature hikes that unveil the wild beauty of this enthralling town.

Boats Rides

An aquatic journey that takes you beyond the beach awaits you in Pondicherry as the sun sets over the Bay of Bengal, casting golden colors. Boat cruises provide visitors a distinctive viewpoint of the town's coastline charm and a chance to see how urban activity and the peace of the sea can coexist.

A short distance from the town lies Chunnambar Boat House, which is the starting point for some of Pondicherry's most picturesque water activities. Take a boat ride through the tranquil backwaters, which are home to many birds and mangrove trees. A highlight is the boat excursion to Paradise Beach, which offers a private sanctuary for those looking for a peaceful getaway with its golden dunes and turquoise seas.

Consider taking a boat to the gorgeous Ousteri Lake for a little taste of cultural adventure. The lake offers a tranquil setting for a boat trip through the symphony of nature, serving as an important habitat for migrating species. The sound of rustling foliage and far-off bird sounds envelops you as you glide over the placid waters, immersing you in the essence of Pondicherry's natural marvels.

Tours by Cycling

It's ideal to explore Pondicherry's charming streets on two wheels, since they are lined with colorful marketplaces and colonial buildings. Cycling excursions enable you to bike around the town's nooks and crannies at a leisurely pace, providing a great combination of adventure and cultural immersion.

Take a bike rental and ride around the French Quarter, where pastel-colored buildings and boulevards dotted with trees will take you back in time. Discover beautiful shops, art galleries, and secret cafés as you meander through the maze-like alleyways. Riding a bike enables you to enjoy the town's laid-back vibe, stopping to take pictures for Instagram or have a freshly made cup of coffee at a wayside café.

For those with a daring streak, take a bicycle journey to see the beautiful countryside outside the municipal boundaries. As you bike past charming towns, verdant paddy fields, and winding pathways, the scenery changes. Talk to the people, enjoy the tranquility of country living, and see the vivid colors of Pondicherry's countryside come to life.

Nature Walks

The natural splendor of Pondicherry transcends its beaches and cityscape. Discovering secret paths and tranquil settings that are sometimes missed by the uninitiated spectator, nature walks provide an opportunity to fully engage with the town's biodiversity.

The Ousteri Wetland and National Park, a sanctuary for nature lovers and birdwatchers, is reached by one such adventure. You may explore the park's many habitats on guided nature walks and see migrating birds, butterflies, and native plants. It's the ideal place to get away from the busy town because of the peaceful atmosphere created by the soft rustling of the leaves and the sporadic call of a faraway bird.

Another peaceful haven for strolls in the outdoors is the 19th-century Botanical Gardens. Wander along roads lined with trees, discover themed gardens, and be in awe of unusual plant life. In addition to providing a breath of fresh air, the gardens show how committed Pondicherry is to protecting its natural heritage.

Utilitarian Advice for Outdoor Adventures

1. Weather Preparedness: To guarantee a pleasant and safe experience, check the weather before starting any outside activity.

2. Guided Tours: To learn more about the area flora, wildlife, and cultural history, take into account choosing guided boat cruises, bike tours, or nature walks.

3. Safety Measures: Put on the proper protective clothing, particularly while going on bike trips. A fun ride requires both comfortable gear and a helmet.

4. Water and Snacks: Bring small snacks and water to remain hydrated when engaging in outdoor activities, particularly in the warmer months.

5. Respect for Nature: Engage in responsible tourism by keeping an eye on approved pathways, showing consideration for the environment, and not upsetting the local fauna.

The outdoor experiences in Pondicherry provide more than simply physical challenge; they serve as a springboard for an immersive journey that blends study of the local environment, cultural immersion, and the simple delight of being outside. As you explore the town's numerous landscapes, the Pondicherry Travel Guide 2024 may serve as your guide. Discover the excitement of boat excursions, the leisurely pace of bike tours, and the tranquility of nature walks that together weave an outdoor tapestry as rich and varied as Pondicherry itself.

RETAIL THERAPY IN PONDICHERRY

Making Your Way Through the Markets and Boutiques

With its unique fusion of cultural influences, Pondicherry provides a shopping experience that is just as varied as the town itself. Discover the colorful markets, quaint shops, and busy bazaars that make Pondicherry a shoppers' paradise in the shopping and markets chapter of The Pondicherry Travel Guide 2024.

Boutique Shops

Boutique shops showcasing Pondicherry's distinctive blend of French and South Indian styles line the town's streets. Nestled among buildings dating back to the colonial period, these boutiques provide a carefully chosen range of artisan goods, clothing, and home décor that showcase Pondicherry's diverse cultural background.

Discover the charming Cluny needlework Centre, renowned for its beautiful hand-stitched needlework. These talented craftspeople paint beautiful patterns on a range of textiles, such as household linens, scarves, and sarees. In addition to providing a chance to buy one-of-a-kind handmade items, the center gives information about the age-old embroidery skills that have been handed down through the centuries.

Kalki Fashion is a must-visit store for people looking for modern designs with a hint of Pondicherry's charm. This chic store offers a variety of clothes, including accessories and fusion wear that combine cutting-edge design with time-honored workmanship. Every garment tells a tale by fusing the town's own cultural flare with worldwide fashion inspirations.

Customary Marketplaces

Goubert Market is a bustling marketplace that perfectly encapsulates Pondicherry's native way of life. It is situated close to the well-known Promenade Beach. There is a kaleidoscope of colors, smells, and noises at the bustling market. The little lanes are lined with vendors offering a variety of goods, including handicrafts, souvenirs, and fresh fruit.

You'll come across a variety of handcrafted soaps, fragrant oils, and traditional South Indian spices as you make your way around the booths. For those who want to bring a little of Pondicherry's culinary and health legacy home with them, the market is a veritable gold mine. You may also get fully immersed in the creative heritage of the town by looking at the colorful exhibition of handicrafts, which includes fabrics, beads, and ceramics.

Shops in the French Quarter

A distinctive shopping experience is created by the French Quarter's colonial buildings and cobblestone streets. Boutiques housed in historic structures provide a variety of French-inspired goods, such as clothing and home décor.

Casablanca is a store renowned for its unique assortment of clothing and accessories, and it is one such jewel. The shop offers a variety that appeals to both fashion fans and those looking for classic items, expertly fusing French fashion inspirations with a hint of Indian workmanship.

The French Quarter's major retail avenues, Rue Saint Gilles and Rue Romain Rolland, are lined with a variety of antique stores, galleries, and lifestyle boutiques. These businesses demonstrate the town's dedication to maintaining its colonial heritage while embracing a contemporary, international atmosphere.

Mission Street shopping options

A haven for window shoppers is Mission Street, a busy road in the center of Pondicherry. Numerous stores along this bustling boulevard offer everything from fashionable accessories to traditional Indian clothing. You may discover both well-established stores and street-side merchants in this melting pot of ethnicities and styles.

Discover the colorful selection of leather products or the South Indian textile legacy of Chettinad cotton sarees. Mission Street is a great place to discover Pondicherry's unique retail scene since it combines traditional and modern elements.

Useful Shopping Advice

1. Bargaining: Bargaining is a typical activity while purchasing on the street. Please feel free to haggle over rates, particularly in small towns.

2. Cash and Cards: Make sure you have both cash and cards on hand since smaller businesses could only accept cash.

3. Local Artists: By buying handcrafted and traditional goods, you may help support your community's artists and craftspeople.

4. Explore Offbeat Streets: Go off the major retail thoroughfares in search of unusual treasures and undiscovered jewels.

5. Cultural Sensitivity: When shopping for traditional things, particularly at markets and shops with a cultural bent, respect local customs and traditions.

The retail scene in Pondicherry offers a tour through the town's artistic, cultural, and historical legacy in addition to the opportunity to purchase things. Whether strolling through the narrow lanes of Goubert Market, perusing boutiques in the French Quarter, or enjoying some retail therapy on Mission Street, every place you visit adds to the complex story that characterizes Pondicherry's distinct personality. As you explore the town's many markets and shops, let the Pondicherry Travel Guide 2024 be your guide to make sure your shopping trip is an unforgettable part of your Pondicherry experience.

PONDICHERRY'S PRACTICAL TIPS

Useful Advice for a Smooth Cruise

A trip to Pondicherry promises to be a lovely mix of adventure, culture, and leisure. The Pondicherry Travel Guide 2024 provides helpful advice to make the most of your trip and guarantee a hassle-free, unforgettable experience.

1. Awareness of the Weather: Pondicherry has a tropical climate, which is defined by warm, muggy days. Check the weather forecast before packing your bags so you are ready for the conditions that will be there. Wearing a hat, sunscreen, and light, breathable clothing is recommended, particularly if you intend to visit beaches and other outdoor attractions.

2. Cultural Respect: It is very important to respect regional traditions and customs. Modest clothing is appreciated when visiting temples, churches, or other places of worship. Remember that some holy locations have limitations on taking pictures. Getting to know and appreciate the local way of life enhances your trip in general.

3. Transportation Choices: There are several ways to get around Pondicherry, such as bicycles, scooter rentals, and auto rickshaws. Depending on your tastes and the distance you intend to travel, select your mode of transportation. When traveling short distances, auto rickshaws are practical, but bicycles and scooters provide more freedom when touring the town and its surroundings.

4. Language Factors: Tamil and French are widely spoken in Pondicherry, even though many residents speak English. Acquiring a few fundamental words in these languages may improve communication and show that you are aware of and respectful of local customs. Positive interactions can be greatly enhanced by using basic greetings and expressions.

5. Currency and Payments: The currency used in Pondicherry is the Indian Rupee. Ensure you have a mix of cash for smaller establishments and cards for larger transactions. ATMs are available in the town, providing easy access to cash when needed.

6. Medical Precautions: Prioritize your health by carrying a basic first aid kit with essentials like pain relievers, band-aids, and any necessary prescription medications. Stay hydrated, particularly in the heated temperature, and consider travel insurance for extra peace of mind.

7. Local Cuisine Exploration: Pondicherry is a sanctuary for food connoisseurs, providing a diversified gastronomic environment. Venture beyond traditional cuisine and experience local delights. Street food booths and traditional restaurants give unique experiences, but check that the sanitary standards fit with your comfort level.

8. Safety Measures: Although Pondicherry is usually seen to be secure for visitors, it's always a good idea to use common sense care. Be watchful of your possessions, particularly in busy locations, and steer clear of dark, uncharted passageways at night. Reputable lodgings may provide further advice on regional safety precautions.

9. Connectivity and Wi-Fi: The majority of Pondicherry's hotels, cafés, and public areas have Wi-Fi available. Still, it's best to have a local SIM card for mobile data so you can remain connected while exploring. Budget-friendly data plans are available from local carriers for the length of your visit.

10. Make a Schedule for Local Events: Pondicherry has a number of events all year long, each of which gives the town a distinct cultural character. Prior to your visit, check the schedule of local festivals and think about scheduling your trip around these events for a more immersive experience. The streets come alive with enthusiasm during festivals like Pongal and Bastille Day.

11. Management of Waste: Make a responsible tourist contribution by putting your trash in the appropriate containers. Pondicherry places a strong emphasis on cleanliness, and little things like disposing of rubbish properly add to the town's allure.

12. Discover Areas Not Often Visited: Even while popular sights are a must-see, don't be afraid to explore less-traveled locations. For a more genuine experience, visit hidden cafés, tiny markets, and unusual alleyways that often show Pondicherry's actual nature.

13. When You Should Visit: Certain attractions, particularly spiritual locations, could have limited hours of operation or occasional events. To make the most of your trip and see any cultural or religious rituals that add to the experience, schedule your visits appropriately.

14. Involve Locals: One of the best things about Pondicherrians is how kind they are. Talk to people, ask for advice, and enjoy the laid-back vibe that gives your trip a more intimate feel.

15. Adaptable Schedule: Plan ahead, but also leave room for improvisation. The attraction of Pondicherry is found in its unanticipated discoveries and spontaneous moments. Give your schedule enough leeway so you may truly experience the town's charm.

Pondicherry, all things considered, provides a tasteful fusion of culture, history, and scenic beauty. If you follow these useful suggestions, you'll not only find it easier to go about the area but also be able to have a more genuine and fulfilling trip. Make the Pondicherry Travel Guide 2024 your reliable travel companion as you set out to see this alluring seaside town in a smooth and unforgettable manner.

FESTIVALS AND EVENTS

Honoring Pondicherry's Cultural Rainbow

The lively festivals and activities that take place in the heart of Pondicherry vibrate with the spirit of celebration, creating a tapestry of colors, customs, and social delight. With each festival serving as a distinct showcase for Pondicherry's many cultural offerings, The Pondicherry Travel Guide 2024 cordially extends an invitation for you to get fully engaged in the vibrant town calendar.

Festival of Pongal

Pongal, an agricultural holiday observed in January, is a time to express thankfulness for the harvest. The town comes alive with celebratory zeal as the scent of freshly cooked Pongal rice fills the air. While preparing the traditional food, families get together to give gratitude to the sun deity for abundant harvests. The streets resound with music, laughing, and the rhythms of traditional drums, all decked with vibrant kolams (rangoli).

Global Yoga Gathering

The International Yoga Festival held in Pondicherry is a sanctuary for those in search of spiritual renewal. This international gathering of yoga practitioners, aficionados, and seekers of spirituality takes place in February. Renowned yoga instructors provide yoga lessons, meditation, and seminars against the beautiful background of Pondicherry's beaches and landscapes. The event showcases holistic health and affirms Pondicherry's standing as a center for spiritual inquiry.

Masi Magam

The holy Hindu festival of Masi Magam, which takes place in February or March, brings together spirituality and Pondicherry's scenic shoreline. In the middle of the town, at the revered Manakula Vinayagar Temple, devotees assemble to take part in a magnificent parade. Deity idols are submerged in the water, and a parade with traditional music and dancing makes its way through the lively streets. Masi Magam embodies the town's spiritual core by merging historic customs with the tranquil atmosphere of its seaside setting.

Bastille Day

Pleasurably honoring its French colonial past, Pondicherry celebrates Bastille Day on July 14. There are parades, cultural events, and delicious food as the French Quarter comes to life. The festival is attended by both locals and visitors, evoking a mood reminiscent of the joie de vivre of France. The celebration centers on the famous Rock Beach and Goubert Avenue, where "Vive la France" reverberates as the tricolor flag is flown with pride.

Sri Aurobindo's Birthday

In addition to being India's Independence Day, August 15th is also Sri Aurobindo's birthday—a highly regarded philosopher and spiritual guide. To commemorate his teachings and legacy, the Pondicherry spiritual center, the Aurobindo Ashram, holds unique activities. At the ashram, devotees and guests congregate for cultural events, spiritual talks, and meditations. There's an air of introspection, thankfulness, and a group effort to find inner tranquility.

Durga Puja and Navratri

In Pondicherry, people celebrate the Hindu holiday of Navaratri, which honors the goddess Durga, with considerable enthusiasm. The lavish decorations, traditional music, and dancing bring the town's temples and homes to life. Vijayadashami, the ninth day, is marked with processions bringing goddess Durga statues to be submerged in the sea. The sounds of drums and the fervor of followers fill the streets, producing a spectacle of adoration and vibrant culture.

New Year's Eve and Christmas

At Christmas, the French Quarter is transformed into a wintry paradise complete with glittering lights, festive décor, and the sound of carols. The community celebrates until New Year's Eve, saying goodbye to the past and welcoming the future with vibrant street gatherings, live music, and fireworks. These festivities have a distinct Pondicherrian character because of the fusion of French and Indian elements.

Auroville Foundation Day

On February 28th, Auroville, an experimental community near Pondicherry, celebrates its founding day. This day commemorates the founding of Auroville in 1968. Cultural concerts, exhibits, and social gatherings are all part of the festivities. The town's dedication to spiritual discovery, ecological living, and human harmony is reflected in Auroville Foundation Day.

Fête de la Musique

Fans of music celebrate the annual Fête de la Musique, a worldwide music festival. This festival in Pondicherry features a variety of musical genres performed by both local and foreign performers. Live music transforms the French Quarter into a stage, creating a peaceful ambiance that reflects the town's multicultural vibe.

Maasi Theertham

During the Maasi Theertham festival, which takes place in February or March, participants take a ceremonial bath at the holy waterfront. At the Promenade Beach, devotees congregate to partake in a sacred sea bath in the hopes of receiving blessings for spiritual cleansing. The beach becomes a destination of pilgrimage, festooned with vivid colors, customs, and an intense feeling of spiritual devotion.

Surging Sea

An annual event held in January called Surging Seas delves at the intersection of environmental awareness and artistic expression. Together, environmentalists and artists produce performances and installations that spread awareness of climate change and its effects on coastal communities. This event is in line with Pondicherry's dedication to environmental preservation and sustainable living.

Karthigai Deepam

Karthigai Deepam is celebrated in the Tamil month of Karthigai (November–December), when many lights light up the town. Oil lamps are used to decorate homes and temples, giving them a cozy and spiritual atmosphere. During this event, the Arunachaleswarar Temple, a well-known spiritual destination in Pondicherry, conducts unique ceremonies and processions.

Film Festival

A wide variety of cinematic works are shown in Pondicherry's film festivals. These gatherings draw fans, cinephiles, and filmmakers and provide a forum for cross-cultural dialogue and a respect for the craft of cinema. Festivals often include talks, films, and Q&A sessions with filmmakers.

Heritage Festival of Ponticherry

The town's architectural and cultural past is celebrated during the annual January Pondicherry Heritage Festival. The festival features activities that showcase

Pondicherry's distinct fusion of French and Indian traditions, including history tours and historians' speeches. The town's history, colonial architecture, and cultural development are all revealed to participants.

Cultural Exhibitions and Workshops for Culture

Pondicherry has artisan fairs, art exhibits, and cultural activities all year round. Local artisans, craftspeople, and cultural aficionados may display their abilities on these platforms. In addition to learning traditional crafts and participating in hands-on activities, visitors may enjoy Pondicherry's varied range of creative expressions.

Utilitarian Advice for Attending Festivals

1. Plan in Advance: Prior to visiting, check the festival schedule to make sure your schedule coincides with activities you're interested in.

2. Room Reservations: Reservations for lodging may fill up rapidly during the busiest festival periods. To guarantee your stay, make bookings ahead of time.

3. Cultural Sensitivity: Observe regional traditions and customs while celebrating religious holidays. Respect the organizers' particular instructions and dress modestly.

4. Exploring Local Cuisine: Festivals often provide unique gastronomic treats. Seize the chance to sample regional specialties and customary celebratory meals.

5. Transportation Considerations: When making travel plans to and from festival locations, keep in mind the possibility of heavy traffic and a surge in attendees during busy hours.

You're not only seeing festivities when you attend Pondicherry's festivals and events; you're also becoming a part of the town's ongoing cultural legacy. Every celebration and event adds to Pondicherry's colorful cultural tapestry, beckoning you to revel, contemplate, and create enduring memories in our refuge by the sea. Enjoy the company of the Pondicherry Travel Guide 2024 as you meander around the lively beats of this captivating town.

DAY ADVENTURE FROM PONDICHERRY

Venturing Past Pondicherry's Edge

A day trip to Pondicherry becomes a doorway to explore the rich tapestry of its surroundings as its appeal draws you beyond its quaint boundaries. The Pondicherry Travel Guide 2024 offers a plethora of options for a day excursion that will never be forgotten, with historical monuments, scenic locales, and cultural treasures waiting just beyond the town limits.

Arikamedu: Piecing Together Old Tales

Visit the archeological site of Arikamedu, which is just a short drive from Pondicherry, to take a trip through time. This historic Roman commerce hub, which dates to the first century BCE, is rich in background. Explore the remains, where artifacts and amphorae relics recount tales of marine commerce and cultural interactions between ancient Rome and the Tamil people. Arikamedu provides an intriguing look at Pondicherry's historical significance as a crossroads.

Island of Paradise Beach: A Tropical Sanctuary

Visit Paradise Beach Island for a day filled with relaxation, sun, and beach. This immaculate island, which is just a short boat trip from Chunnambar Boat House, has golden beaches, blue seas, and an abundance of vegetation. Explore the island's natural paths, relax on the beach, or have a swim in the ocean. For a day of leisure, Paradise Beach is the perfect getaway because of its peace and quiet, which stands in sharp contrast to Pondicherry's lively vitality.

Seaside Temples in Mahabalipuram

Travel north on the picturesque East Coast Road, and you will arrive at the ancient town of Mahabalipuram in a few hours. Renowned for its elaborately carved sculptures and ancient rock-cut temples, this UNESCO World Heritage Site is a must-see. Admire the wonders of 7th-century architecture as you explore the Shore Temple, Arjuna's Penance, and the Five Rathas.

Mahabalipuram is a must-see location for a day trip from Pondicherry since it provides an enthralling fusion of spirituality and cultural history.

Chidambaram: Nataraja's Cosmic Dance

Take in the serene atmosphere of Chidambaram, the site of the renowned Nataraja Temple. This town, which is two hours' drive from Pondicherry, is well-known for its historic temple that honors Lord Shiva in the form of his cosmic dance. See the magnificence of the temple's architecture, which is embellished with colorful artwork and detailed sculptures. The Nataraja Temple invites you to feel the holy beat of the cosmic dance. It is not only a place of worship but also a cultural gem.

Pichavaram Mangrove Forest: A Symphony of Nature

The tranquil beauty of Pichavaram Mangrove Forest, only a short drive from Pondicherry, is a haven for nature lovers. Take a boat trip through a system of mangrove-lined canals and experience the peaceful atmosphere of this unusual environment. Offering a cool escape from the hustle and bustle of the city, the mangrove cover's thick cover, varied birds, and the rhythmic lap of water against the boat form a perfect symphony of nature.

Gingee Fort: A Stone Citadel

Go back in time with a trip to Gingee Fort, also known as the "Troy of the East." This magnificent fort is around two hours' drive from Pondicherry and is a reminder of centuries' worth of history. Discover its enormous granaries, fortifications, and citadels. Climb to the top for sweeping views of the surroundings. The architectural magnificence and strategic importance of Gingee Fort provide an insight into the military might of earlier times.

Spiritual Heights: Thiruvannamalai

Known for the Annamalaiyar Temple, Thiruvannamalai is a spiritual refuge tucked away at the foot of the Annamalai Hills. Towering above the town, the temple honoring Lord Shiva draws both pilgrims and seekers. A day excursion to Thiruvannamalai provides the chance to take in the town's ethereal spiritual atmosphere, visit the temple's expansive complex, and ascend the holy Arunachala Hill.

Helpful Advice for Day Trips

1. Early Departure: Get out early on your day excursion to maximize the sights and steer clear of the noon heat and congestion.

2. Comfortable Attire: Dress comfortably and wear appropriate footwear for the activities planned for the day excursion.

3. Water and Snacks: Keep water and small snacks with you at all times to keep hydrated and alert.

4. Local transit: Take into account local transit choices such as cars, buses, or rental vehicles based on your location.

5. Admission Prices and Timings: Make sure to arrange your schedule appropriately by checking the admission prices and timings for each attraction ahead of time.

6. Local Maps and Guides: Bring along local maps or guides to help you navigate, particularly if you're visiting less visited places.

7. Respect for Cultural Sites: Follow clothing regulations and cultural etiquette when you visit historical sites or temples.

8. Weather Considerations: Make sure your plans take into account the weather at the location of your day excursion.

A day excursion from Pondicherry involves an investigation of many landscapes, history, and cultural subtleties rather than merely a tour to neighboring sights. Every day excursion opens a new chapter in the tale of your Pondicherry adventure, whether you decide to explore the spiritual heights of Thiruvannamalai, the serene beauty of Paradise Beach, or the historical allure of Mahabalipuram. Use the Pondicherry Travel Guide 2024 as a guide as you explore the areas outside of the town and find the hidden gems that are just a day's drive away.

ITINERARY SUGGESTIONS

A 3-Day Itinerary for a Memorable Experiences

With its unique combination of spiritual sanctuaries, French colonial beauty, and coastline attraction, Pondicherry entices visitors to go on an exploratory voyage. A well planned three-day schedule is provided by the Pondicherry Travel Guide 2024 to make the most of your trip to this charming seaside town.

First Day: Touring the French Quarter's History

- **A Walk Around White Town in the Morning:** Take a leisurely walk around White Town's cobblestone lanes, which form the center of Pondicherry's French Quarter, to begin your day. Admire the pastel-colored houses, bold bougainvillea covering the façade, and architecture from the colonial period. Experience the town's French heritage by strolling through the quaint cafés and shops that line the streets. See the famous French War Memorial, which

honors troops who fought and died in World War
I.

- **Late Morning: Jesus' Sacred Heart Basilica**:
Visit the Basilica of the Sacred Heart of Jesus, an
architectural wonder that represents the variety of
spiritual beliefs found in Pondicherry. Admire
this Catholic church's tranquil atmosphere and
neo-Gothic architecture. Spend a time amid its
serene environs in silent contemplation.

- **Lunch: French Quarter Café Hopping:** Take a
gastronomic adventure and visit the charming
eateries located in the French Quarter. Savor a
blend of French and South Indian cuisines while
having a leisurely lunch at a rooftop café or a
bistro in the French manner. Le Café, Baker
Street, and Café des Arts are well-liked options.

- **Pondicherry Museum and Bharathi Park in
the afternoon:** Go to the Pondicherry Museum,
which is located in a renovated French colonial

structure. Explore its unique collection of items that highlight the history, culture, and artwork of the area. Take a stroll around Bharathi Park, a tranquil park with fountains, sculptures, and covered walkways. The park offers a peaceful haven in the middle of the busy metropolis.

- **Afternoon: Sunset at Promenade Beach:** Head out to the famous Promenade Beach as the sun starts to set. Take a leisurely walk down the promenade and enjoy the lively ambiance and sea air. Capture the orange and pink colors that appear on the horizon as the sun sets over the Bay of Bengal. With its recognizable Gandhi Statue, the Promenade Beach is the ideal place for a contemplative and leisurely evening.

- **Evening: Dining by the Sea at Le Dupleix**: Finish your day with a delicious meal at the historic hotel Le Dupleix, which has a colonial-era atmosphere. Savor a lavish dinner of French and Creole cuisine while taking in the beauty of this historic location. The eating area in the courtyard gives your evening a romantic touch.

Day 2: Immersion in Culture and Spiritual Exploration

- **Morning: Auroville - City of Dawn**

  Visit Auroville, an experimental community devoted to spiritual discovery and human togetherness, first thing in the morning. Discover the Matrimandir, a marvel of architecture and a representation of the principles of Auroville. Take part in a meditation class or just take in the calm environment. Discover the ecological techniques and creative undertakings on display at the Auroville Visitor's Center.

- **Lunch: Auroville Cafés and Bakeries**

  Enjoy lunch at one of the many cafés in Auroville to get a taste of its unusual eating scene. With an emphasis on organic and locally sourced foods, Tanto Pizzeria, Bread &

Chocolate, and Auroville Bakery provide a variety of gastronomic experiences.

- **Afternoon: Sri Aurobindo Ashram**
Return to Pondicherry and pay a visit to the Sri Aurobindo Ashram, a center of spirituality established by The Mother and Sri Aurobindo. Take a look around the ashram, pay a visit to the Samadhi, and practice silent meditation. The ashram offers a peaceful haven from the outer world because of its peaceful vibe.

- **Evening: Cultural Performances and Beach Meditation**
Come back to Promenade Beach as the day comes to an end for an unforgettable beach meditation experience. Participate in the nighttime meditation sessions with both residents and visitors, enabling the waves' rhythmic sound to further your spiritual development. Investigate the town's cultural activities and shows in the evening. Cultural events, music concerts, and art

exhibits are often held at the Kala Kendra and Alliance Française.

- **Dinner: Villa Shanti's Heritage Dining**
  Finish your day with supper at the beautifully renovated historic Villa Shanti, which serves a blend of Indian and French cuisine. A wonderful environment for an unforgettable dining experience is created by the sophisticated atmosphere and delicious meal.

Day 3: Culinary Delights and a Nature Retreat
- **Morning: Serenity at Ousteri Lake**
  Visit Ousteri Lake, a peaceful freshwater lake a short distance from Pondicherry, to start your day. Take a boat trip through the peaceful backwaters, which are home to migrating birds and lush vegetation. Birdwatchers and nature lovers will find peace and quiet at the lake.

- **Late Morning: Examine Auroville's Eco-Friendly Methods**

Return to Auroville to investigate its green projects. Learn about organic farming, alternative energy sources, and sustainable living by visiting the Auroville Sustainable Practices. Take part in classes or just admire this unique community's eco-friendly initiatives.

- **Lunch: Tanto's Farm Fresh: Farm-to-Table Dining**

  Discover farm-to-table cuisine at Tanto's Farm Fresh, a restaurant located in Auroville. Savor a dish prepared with fresh, regional ingredients to fully experience the tastes of the area.

- **Afternoon: Serenity Beach Beach Retreat**

  Visit Serenity Beach in the afternoon, which is renowned for its immaculate beaches and laid-back atmosphere. Enjoy beach activities, relax by the water, or just take in the peace and quiet of this coastal sanctuary. A more tranquil option to the busy Promenade Beach is Serenity Beach.

- **Evening: Satsanga's Culinary Delights**

  Finish your day with supper at Satsanga, a well-liked eatery with a varied cuisine and a lively atmosphere. Select from a variety of Indian and foreign meals and savor a delicious fusion of tastes. The restaurant often has live music, which livens up your evening.

This three-day journey offers a harmonic fusion of nature, spirituality, history, and gastronomic pleasures, encapsulating the essence of Pondicherry. A compelling place where every day offers fresh discoveries and unforgettable experiences, Pondicherry unfolds as you wander through the French Quarter, meditate in Auroville, or enjoy a sunset by the beach. Enjoy the company of the Pondicherry Travel Guide 2024 as you explore this charming seaside town.

INSIDER TIPS FOR A UNIQUE EXPERIENCE

Discovering Pondicherry's Undiscovered Treasures

While seeing Pondicherry's well-known sites is enjoyable, the real enchantment is found in finding its hidden treasures, the obscure locations frequented by both residents and seasoned tourists. Insider advice is revealed in The Pondicherry Travel Guide 2024 to help you discover the town's distinct charm and make extraordinary moments.

1. Auroville's Secret Garden: Explore Auroville's hidden gardens by going beyond its famous sites. These peaceful nooks of foliage, situated far from the main tourist destinations, provide a calm haven. Discover Matrimandir Gardens, where colorful butterflies create a painting out of the surrounding vegetation. Sit quietly and meditate while admiring the splendor of these undiscovered nature retreats.

2. The Alleyway Art Gallery at Café des Arts: Even though Café des Arts is a well-liked location, you may discover more of its appeal by visiting the nearby alleyway art gallery. The alley walls are often used as canvases by neighborhood artists, producing a dynamic outdoor art display. This secret gallery offers a visual feast that goes beyond your cup of coffee, adding an artistic touch to your café experience.

3. Legal Walk along Rue Romain Rolland: Stroll around Rue Romain Rolland, a historic street, and discover literature beyond the busy stores. Take in the charming bookstores and tucked-away corners where readers congregate. Unplanned poetry readings or conversations might occur, giving your tour of Pondicherry's French Quarter a literary flair.

4. Ritual of Promenade Beach Sunrise: Promenade Beach is a well-liked location for sunsets, but insiders understand that the morning is when its real beauty happens. Come enjoy a peaceful dawn ritual with the locals, where runners, yoga practitioners, and others looking for a quiet moment will intersperse the early morning stillness. Pondicherry has a separate, more private aspect that is shown by the beach at sunrise.

5. Tasmai's Creative Enclave: Explore Tasmai, a less-visited creative haven. Local and international artists provide performances, art installations, and exhibits at this cultural center. Accept Pondicherry's modern art scene, where Tasmai is transformed into a creative canvas that transcends traditional galleries.

6. Walk through the Muslim Quarters with Heritage: Take a history stroll through Pondicherry's less well-known Muslim neighborhood. Explore the charming streets that have colorful facades and classic buildings. Talk to people, explore old mosques, and enjoy the unique cultural fabric that makes up this sometimes-overlooked area of the city.

7. Shopping Secrets for the Pondy Streets Bazaar: Insiders know that the genuine shopping secrets are found in the lesser alleyways of Pondy Streets Bazaar, even if the major marketplaces are humming with activity. Discover tucked-away shops, handmade craft galleries, and family-owned establishments that sell distinctive items. This unique shopping experience reveals gems that add to Pondicherry's eclectic retail scene.

8. The Alternative Cafés in Auroville: Auroville conceals a wealth of other settings; it's not only about the well-known cafés. Look for tucked-away cafés in Auroville's lush surroundings, where you may socialize and savor organic treats. These less well-known locations provide a more personal and genuine Auroville experience.

9. Serenity Beach's Hidden Sunset Spot: Although Serenity Beach is famed for its relaxed atmosphere, insiders know of a hidden location for sunsets. Find a more peaceful area on the beach by straying from the main group of people. You will enjoy a more private and intimate view of the magnificent Serenity Beach sunset as the sun sets.

10. Events in the Kottakuppam Community: A look into real coastal life may be had during community activities held in the adjacent fishing town of Kottakuppam. Look out for fishing events, festivals, and cultural festivities. Interacting with the people offers a unique viewpoint on the mutually beneficial interaction between Pondicherry and its surrounding villages.

11. Arulmigu Manakula Vinayagar Temple Insights: Though it's a well-liked destination, experts advise going during festivals or other special occasions at the Manakula Vinayagar Temple. Experiencing customary rituals and processions enhances the cultural richness of your temple visit. Talk to the priests and residents of the temple to learn more about the spiritual rituals that make it function.

12. The Hidden Backwaters of Ousteri Lake: Insiders investigate Ousteri Lake's undiscovered backwaters, despite the lake being popular for boat tours. Get off the beaten path and explore hidden areas brimming with wildlife and breathtaking scenery. This undiscovered side of Ousteri Lake offers a closer encounter with Pondicherry's natural surroundings.

13. Street Food Secrets of Mission Street: Insiders know that, despite its busy retail district, Mission Street is also a sanctuary for street cuisine. Discover the lesser-known street food carts and stalls and enjoy the frequently overlooked local specialties. Discover the undiscovered gastronomic treasures of Mission Street, ranging from classic sweets to savory nibbles.

14. Nighttime at Rock Beach: Rock Beach is not simply for strolls during the day; at night it becomes an enchanted location. Insiders often visit Rock Beach after dusk, when soothing lights illuminate the promenade. Savor the tranquil appeal, the sound of the waves, and the mild sea air of this famous spot beneath the stars at night.

15. Nearby Craft Centers: Explore Pondicherry's surrounding artisan workshops and go beyond the retail establishments. These secret locations, which range from ceramics studios to classic craft workshops, let you see the artistry that goes into creating the town's distinctive goods. Interact with craftspeople, discover their methods, and bring unique mementos home.

With the help of these insider recommendations, you may uncover Pondicherry's lesser-known areas and secret nooks. By using these insights as a guide, you'll not only discover the town's best-kept secrets but also develop a closer connection with its people, culture, and artwork. As you explore the less-traveled paths in this seaside sanctuary, let the Pondicherry Travel Guide 2024 serve as your guide.

ADDITIONAL RESOURCES AND READING FOR PONDICHERRY VISITORS

You may learn more about Pondicherry's rich history, culture, and distinct charm by exploring other resources when your trip takes you there. A carefully selected selection of materials and further reading is suggested by The Pondicherry Travel Guide 2024 to enhance your investigation and provide insightful perspectives into the complex aspects of this alluring seaside resort.

1. Online resources and guides

- **Official Website for Pondicherry Tourism**: [Official Website for Pondicherry Tourism](https://tourism.puducherry.gov.in/): Offers current information about events, attractions, and useful travel advice.

- Auroville Official Website: Visit [Auroville](https://www.auroville.org/) to learn about the organization's mission, programs, and visitor details.

- PondyLive - Events and Culture: Using this extensive web platform, you can stay up to speed on all the festivals, events, and activities taking place in Pondicherry.

- Pondicherry360 - Virtual Tour: From the convenience of your smartphone, explore Pondicherry's main sights virtually with [Pondicherry360](https://www.pondicherry360.com/).

- Pondicherry history Walks: Take part in guided history walks to discover the town's historical sites and undiscovered treasures. Visit [Pondicherry Heritage Walks](https://www.pondicherryheritagewalks.com/).

2. Movies and Documentaries:

- The Other Side of the Ocean (2007): A documentary examining Pondicherry's distinctive Franco-Tamil culture and the difficulties the locals encounter.

- **Auroville:** The City of the Future: The 2018 documentary exploring the philosophy and way of life of the Auroville community.

- **Bombay Beach (2011)**: Although unrelated to Pondicherry, this documentary stimulates contemplation on deliberate living by providing an insightful viewpoint on society and life.

3. Local Cultural and Art Events:

- **La Galerie d'Art:** Visit La Galerie d'Art, a contemporary art gallery in Pondicherry, to have a deeper understanding of the local art scene.

- **Bharathiyar Palkalaikoodam**: Take part in cultural activities and shows at Bharathiar Palkalaikoodam to improve your knowledge of regional arts.

- **Tasmai Center for Art and Culture**: Discover the many creative expressions in Pondicherry via the exhibits and cultural activities held at Tasmai.

4. Yoga and Spiritual Retreats:

- **Sri Aurobindo Ashram**: To enhance your spiritual experience, participate in meditations, spiritual talks, and cultural activities at the Ashram.

- **International Yoga Festival in Pondicherry**: Take part in the yearly International Yoga Festival to network with internationally recognized yoga instructors and practitioners.

- **Auroville Retreat**: Take into consideration enrolling in an Auroville retreat, which provides a comprehensive yoga, meditation, and wellness experience.

5. Sustainable and Environmental Initiatives:

- **Pitchandikulam Forest**: Auroville's Green Belt: Discover the Pitchandikulam Forest, an endeavor to conserve biodiversity that supports the natural equilibrium of the area.

- **Auroville Sustainable Practices**: Expand your knowledge of environmental awareness by learning about Auroville's sustainable living practices.

- **Surging Seas Festival**: Keep yourself updated on environmental projects such as Surging Seas, an occasion that delves into the relationship between art and consciousness of climate change.

You will get a comprehensive understanding of Pondicherry by exploring these materials, which cover everything from its spiritual significance and environmental efforts to its cultural diversity and historical tapestry. These suggestions are meant to enhance your travels by offering a comprehensive perspective of Pondicherry's history, culture, and future. Use the Pondicherry Travel Guide 2024 as a starting point to delve further about this intriguing seaside town.

Printed in Great Britain
by Amazon

43949638R00046